The Right Way To Draw Dinosaurs

How to Draw Different Types
of Dinosaurs

Dinosaurs

By : Gala Publication

Published By :

Gala Publication

© Copyright 2015 – Gala Publication

ISBN-13: **978-1522708742**
ISBN-10: **152270874X**

Table of Contents

ALLOSAURUS

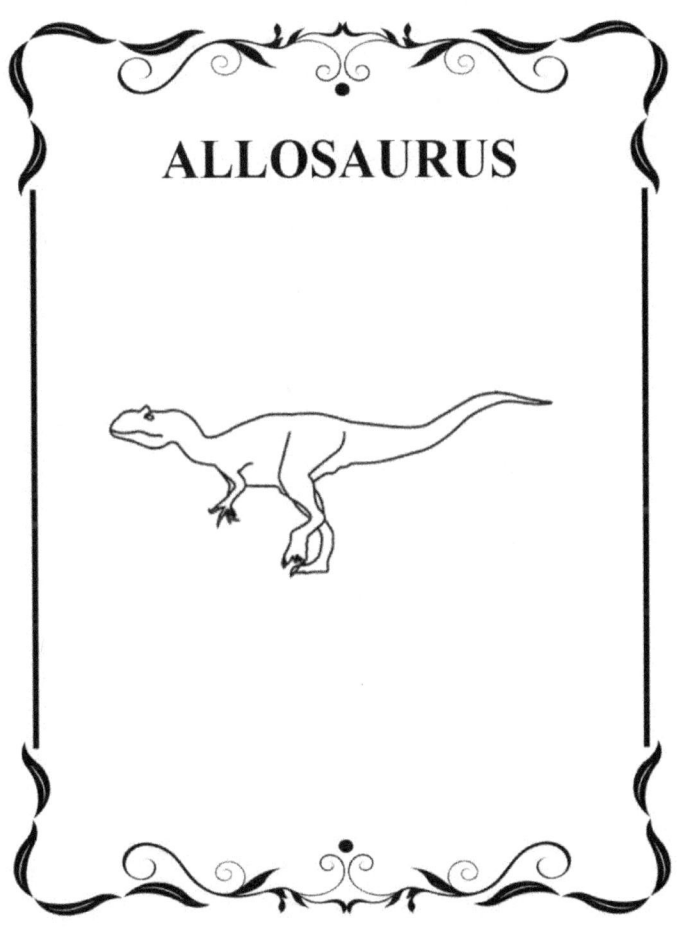

STEP 1

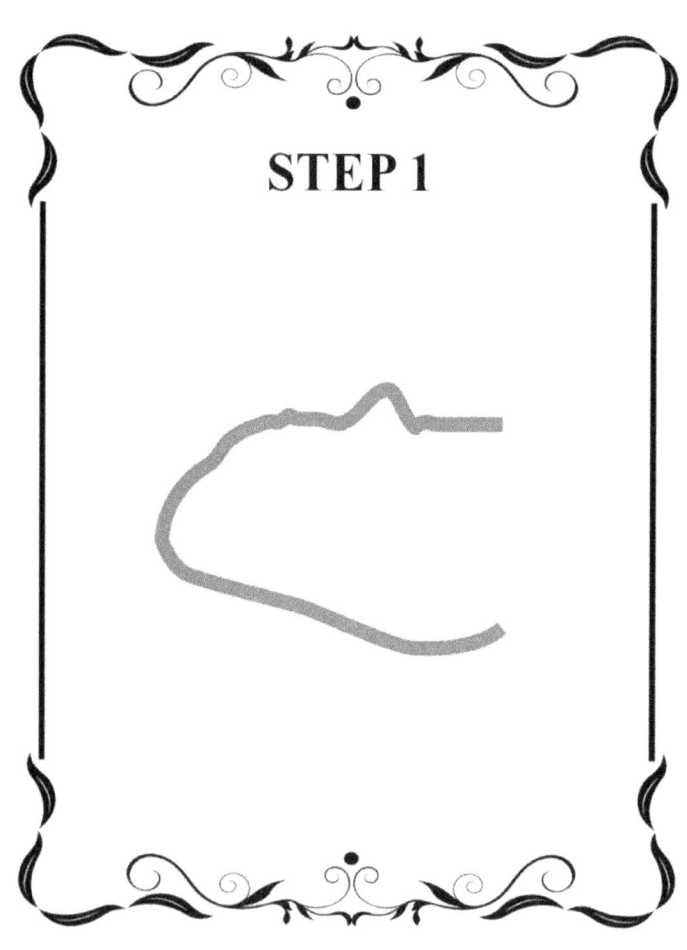

STEP 2

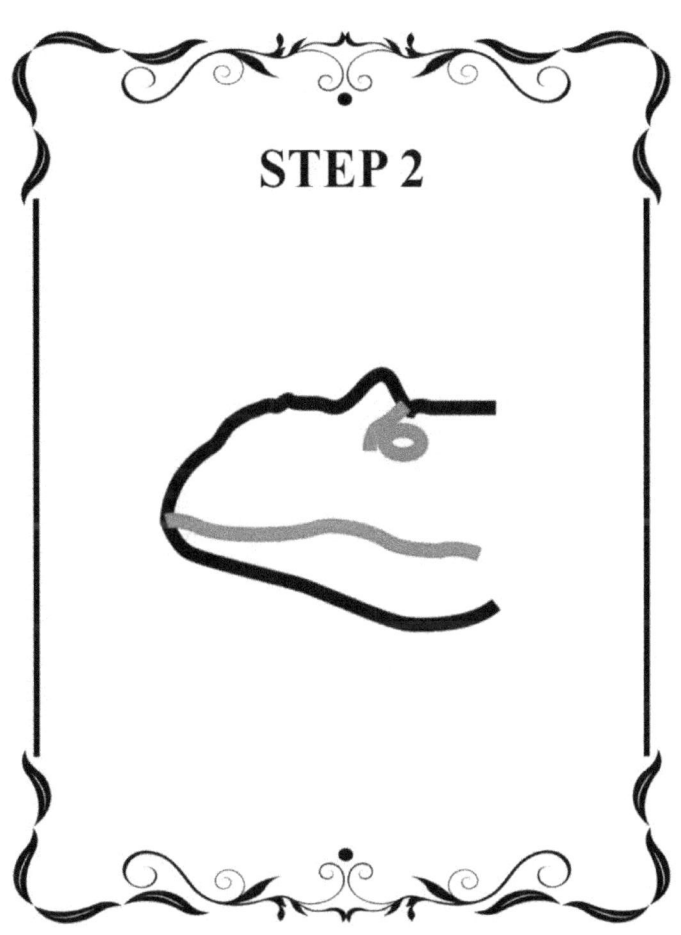

STEP 3

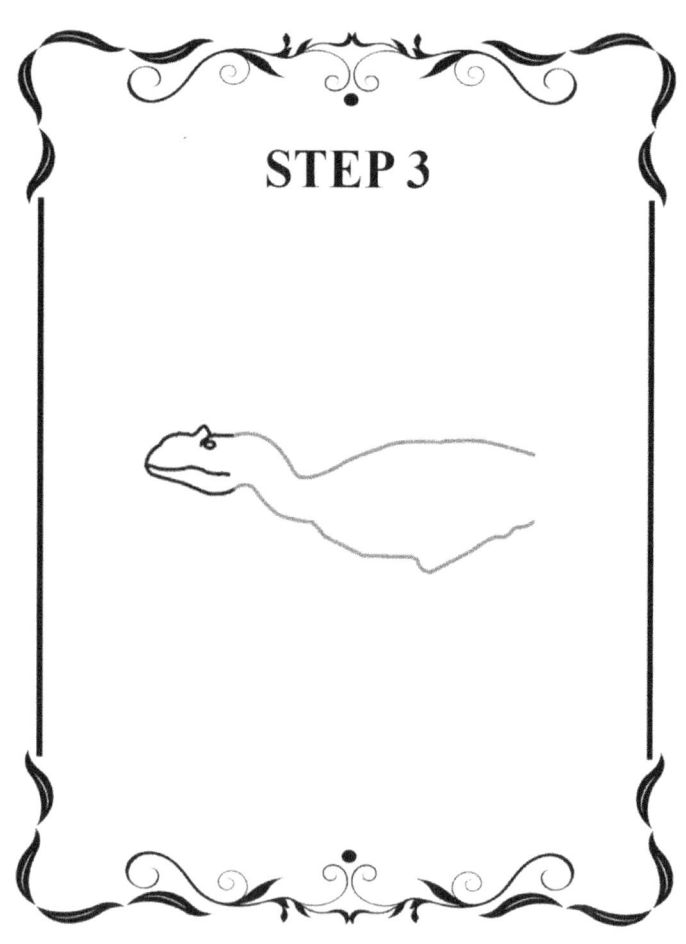

STEP 4

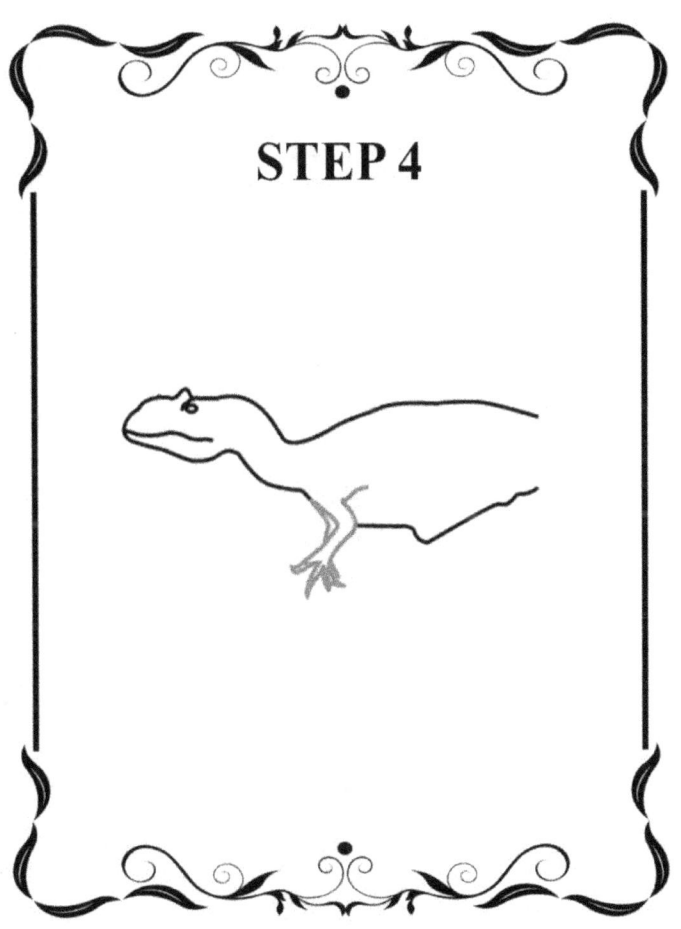

STEP 5

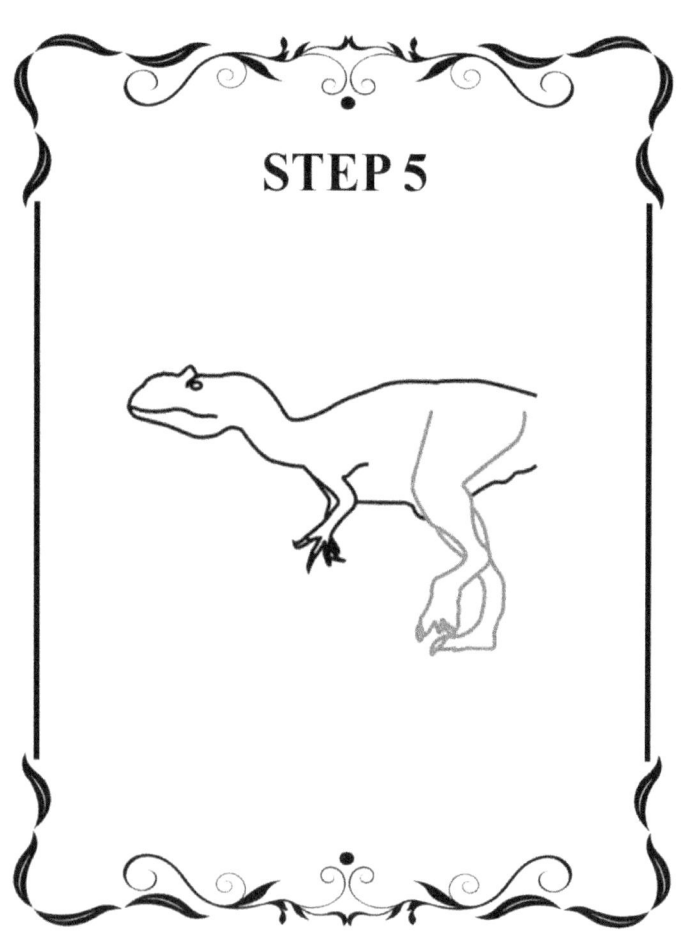

STEP 6

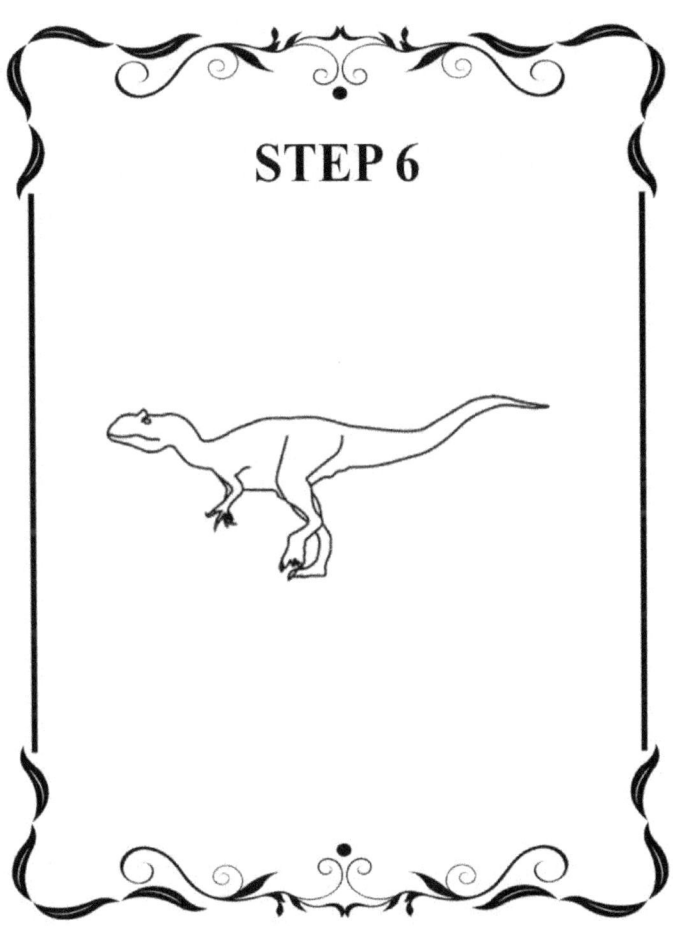

ANKYLOSAURUS

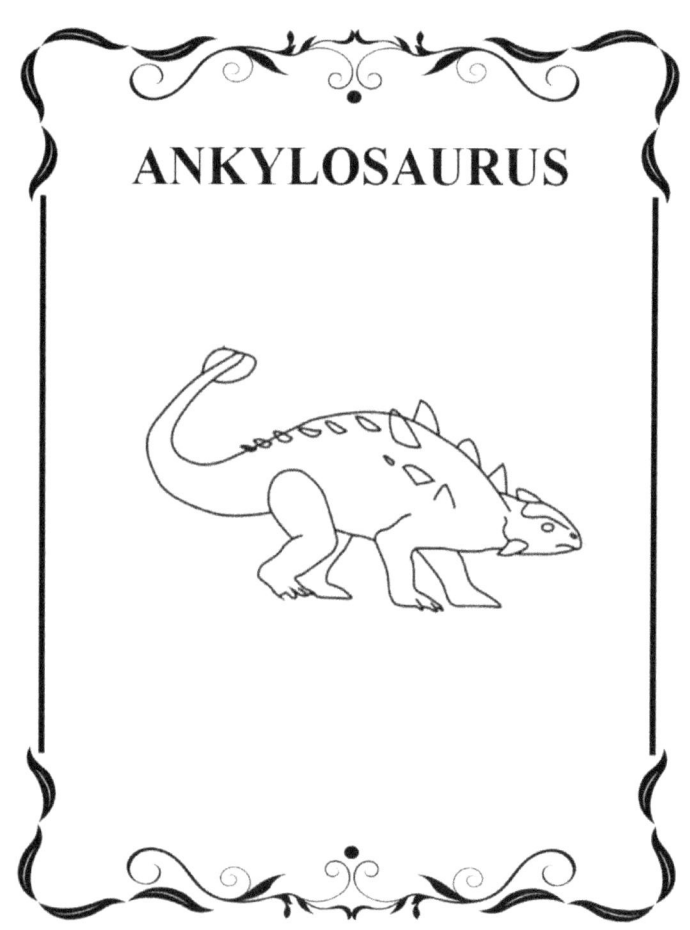

STEP 1

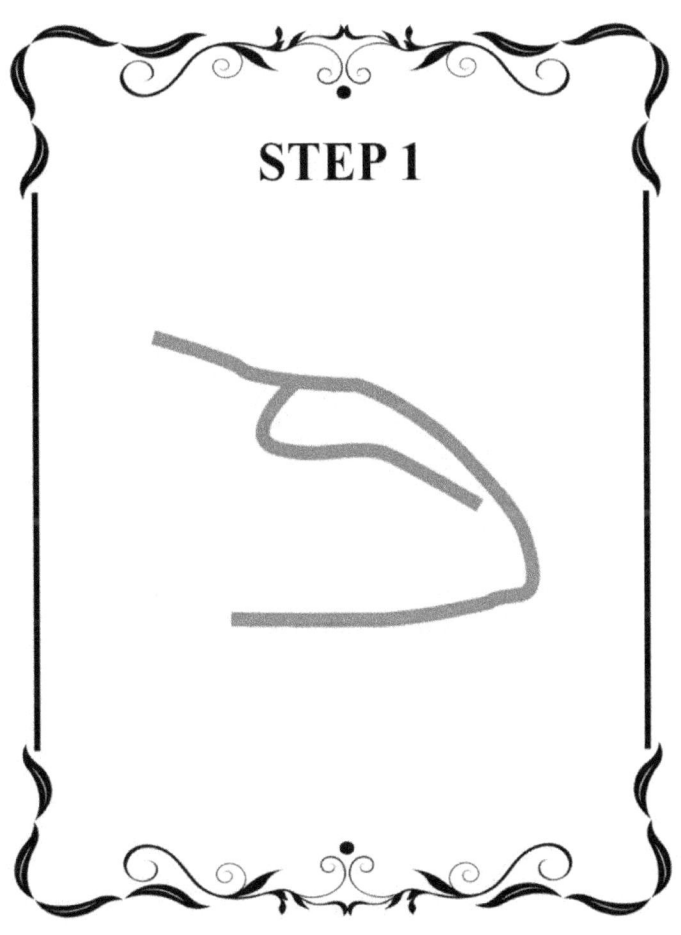

STEP 2

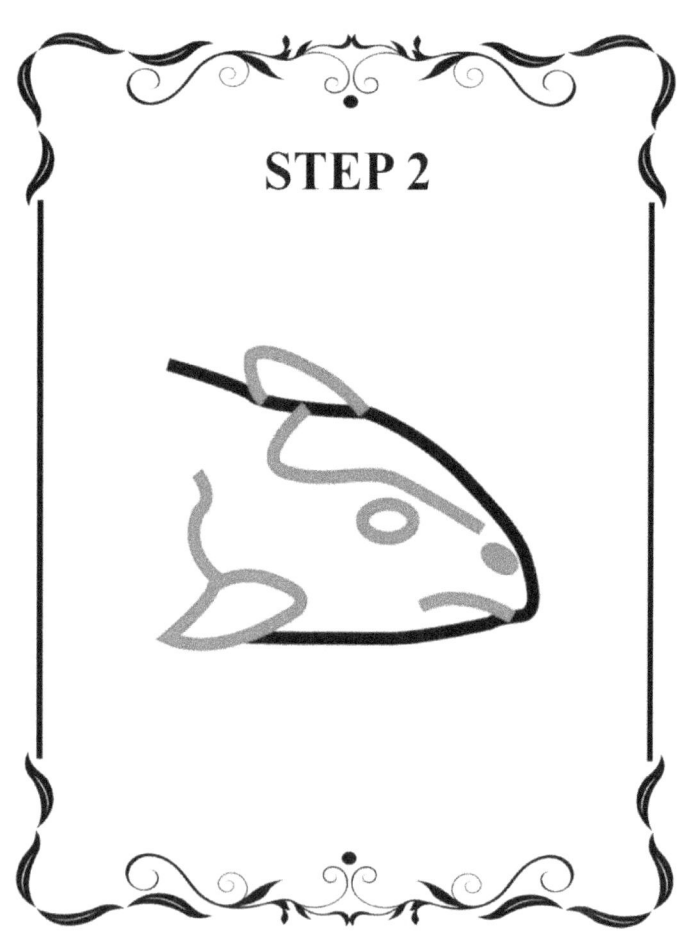

STEP 3

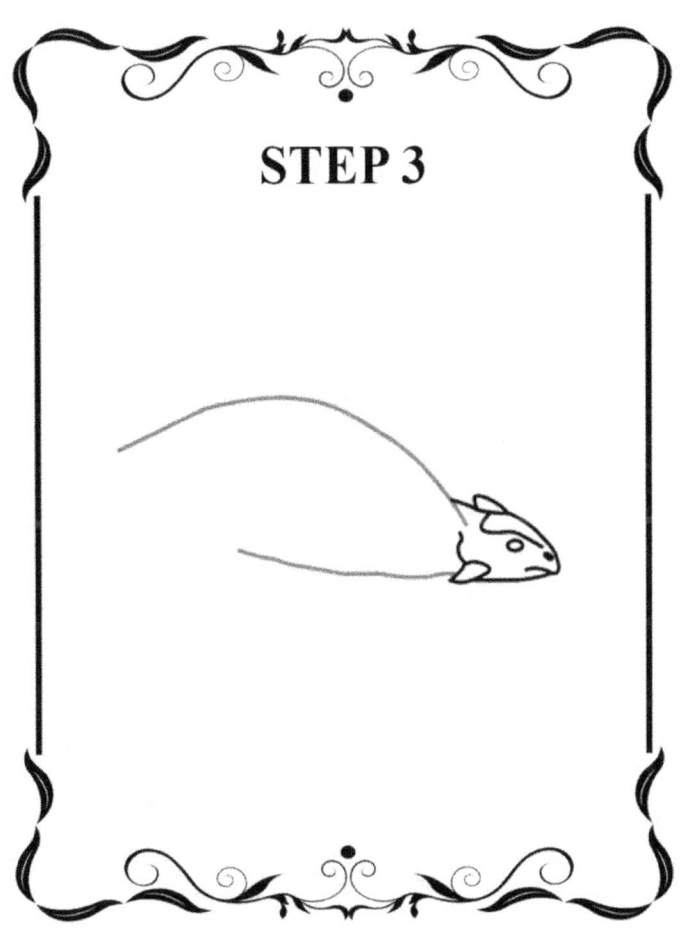

STEP 4

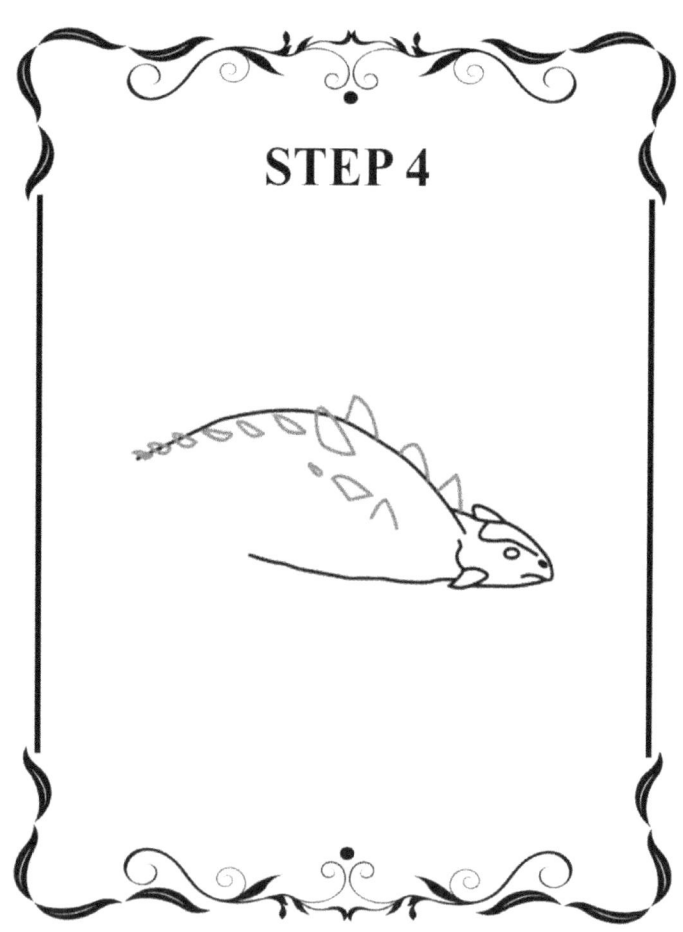

STEP 5

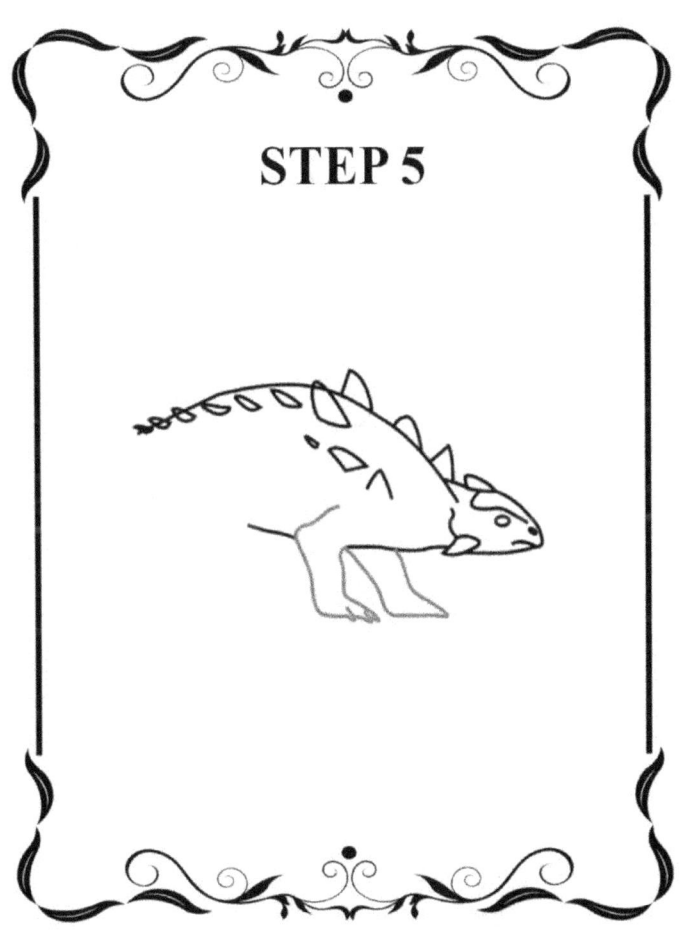

STEP 6

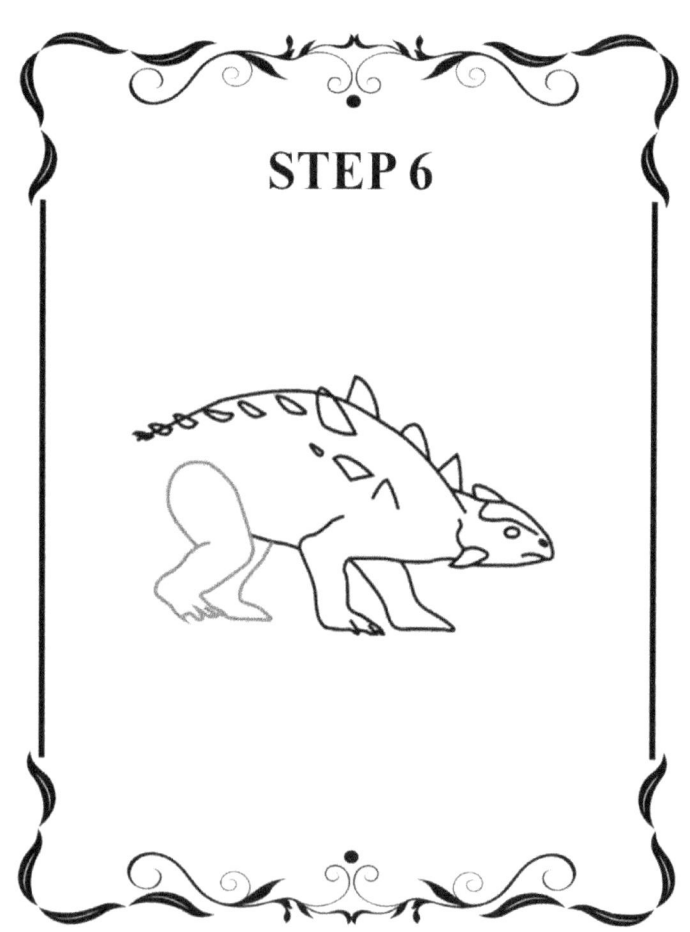

STEP 7

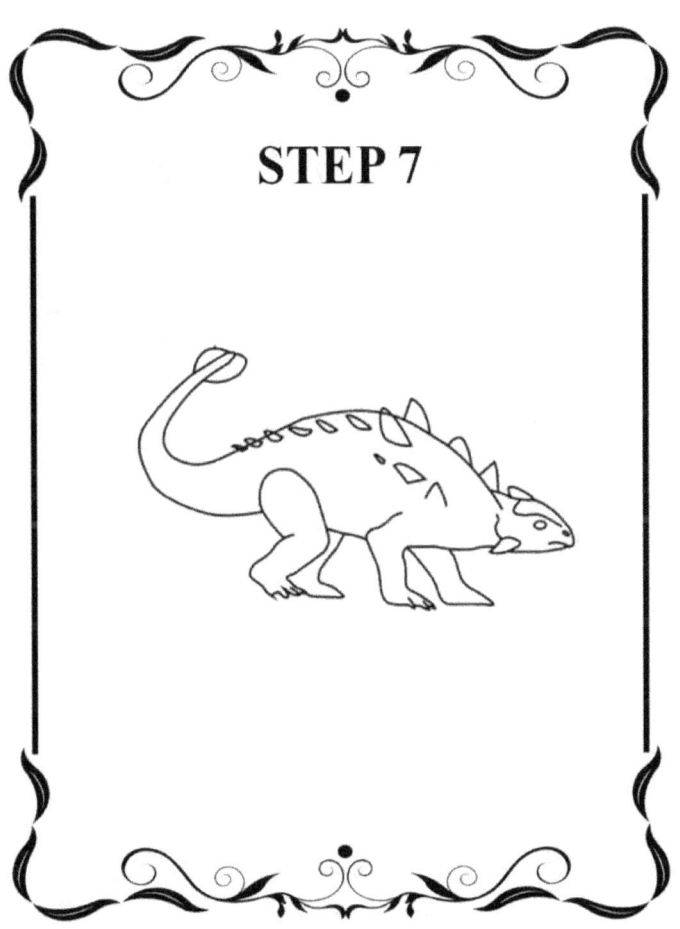

APATOSAURUS

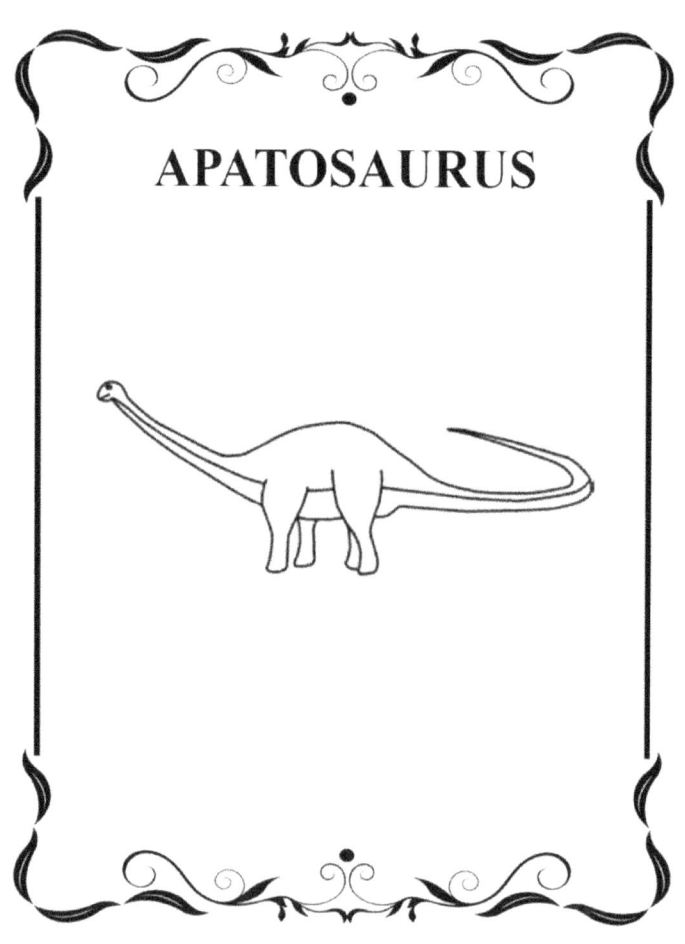

STEP 1

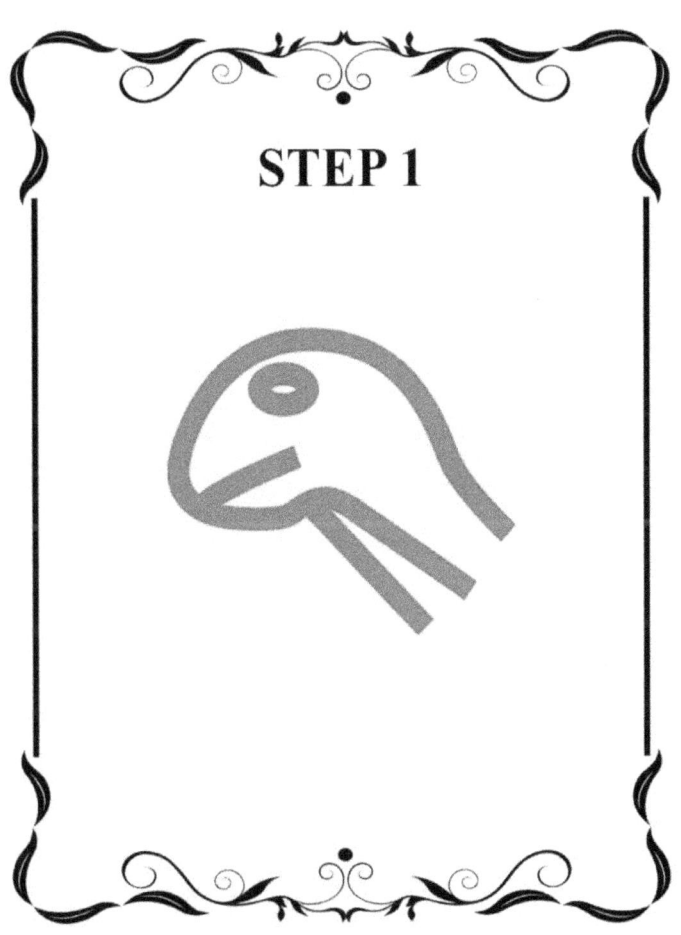

STEP 2

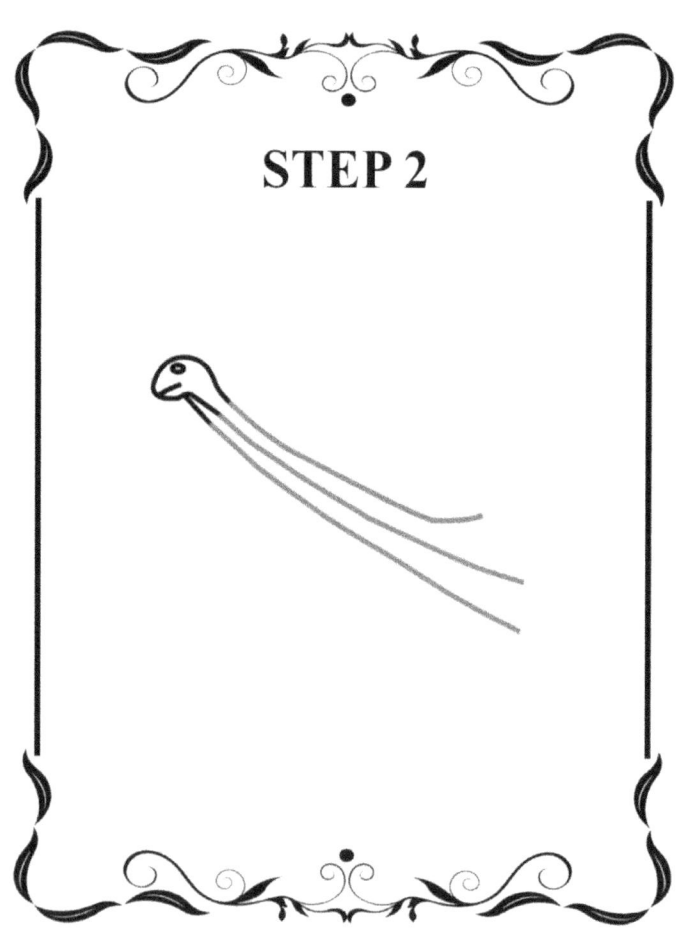

STEP 3

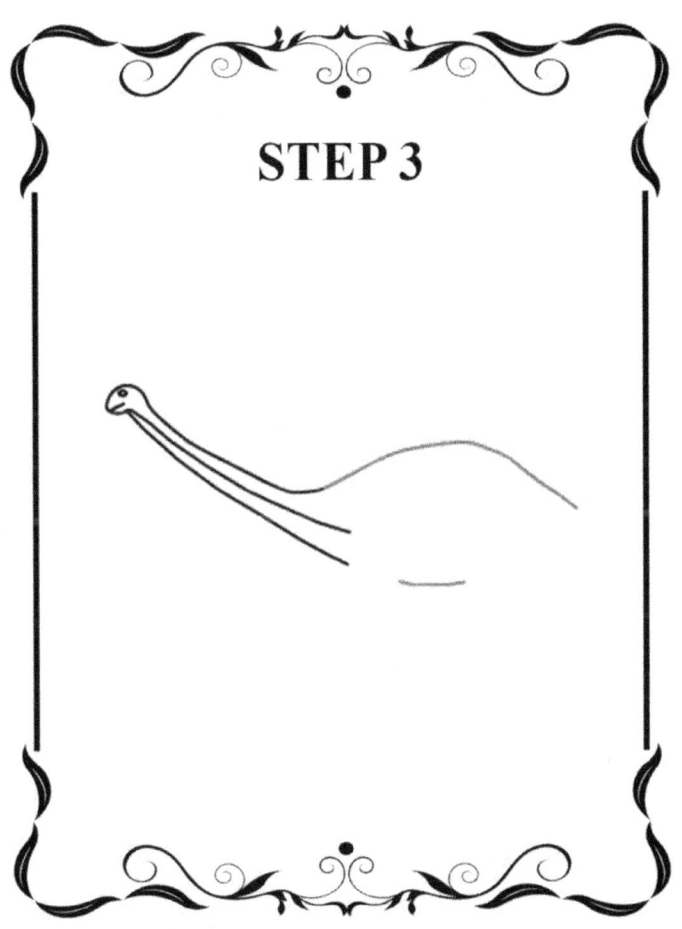

STEP 4

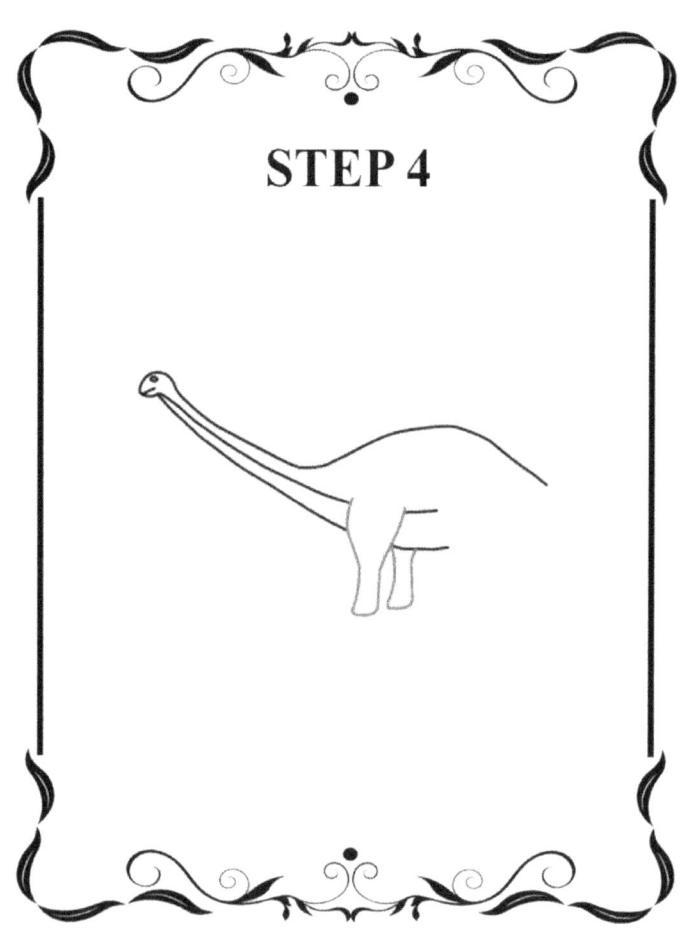

STEP 5

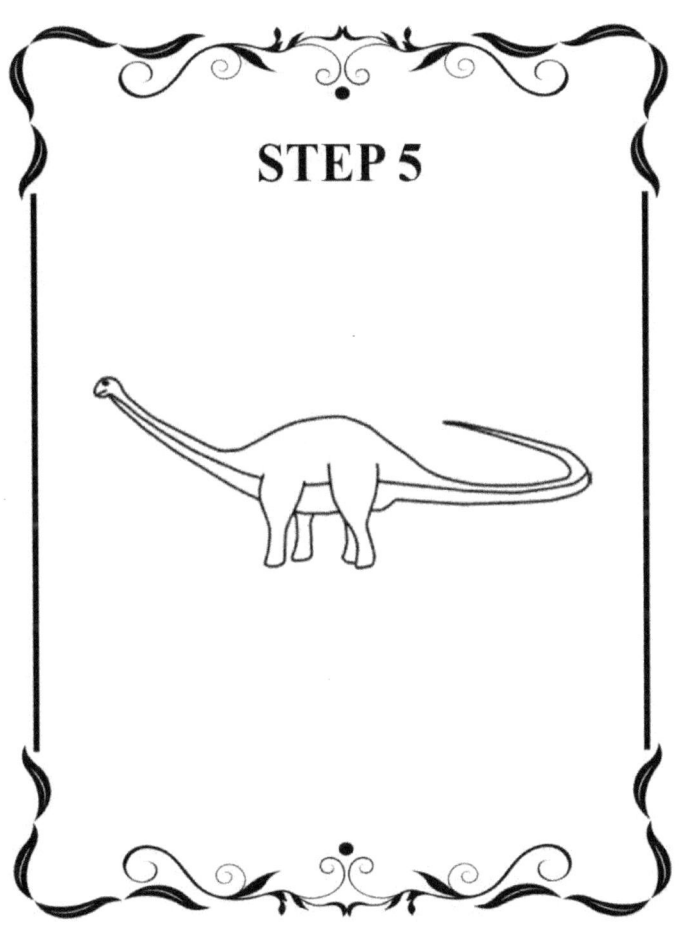

BARYNOYX

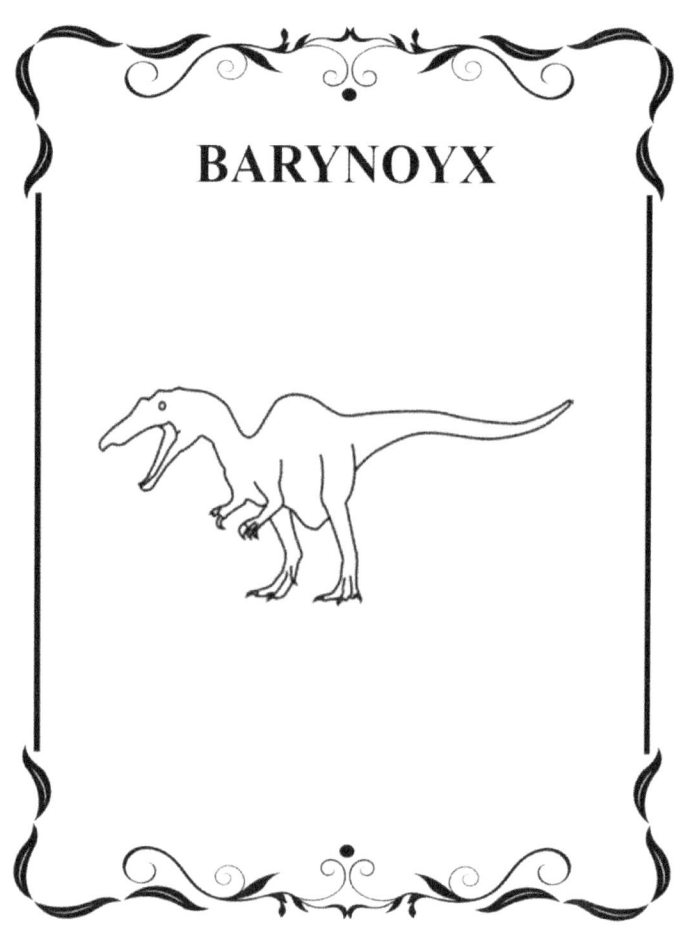

STEP 1

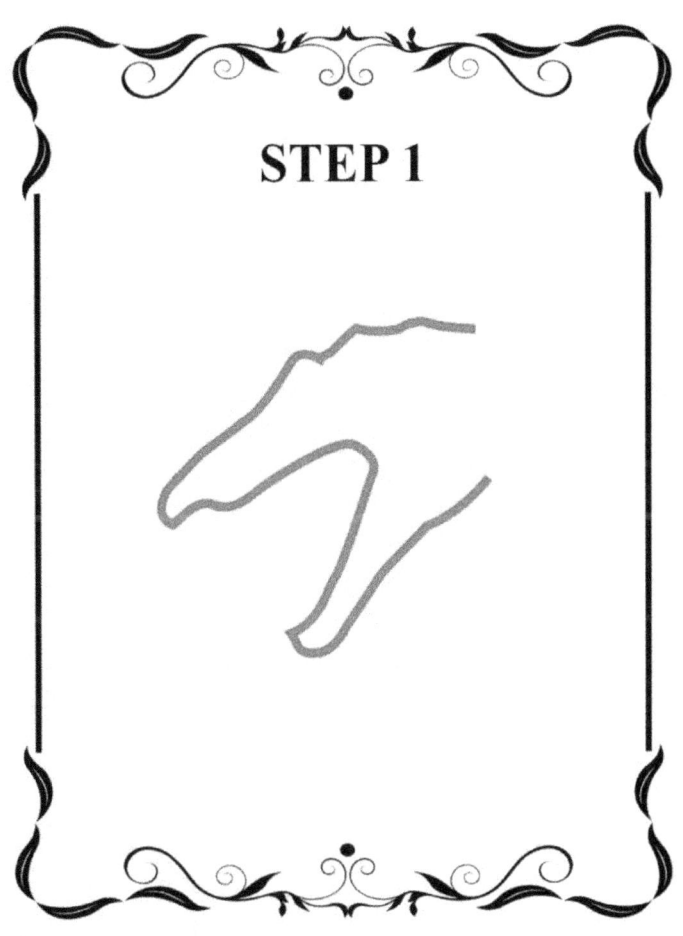

STEP 2

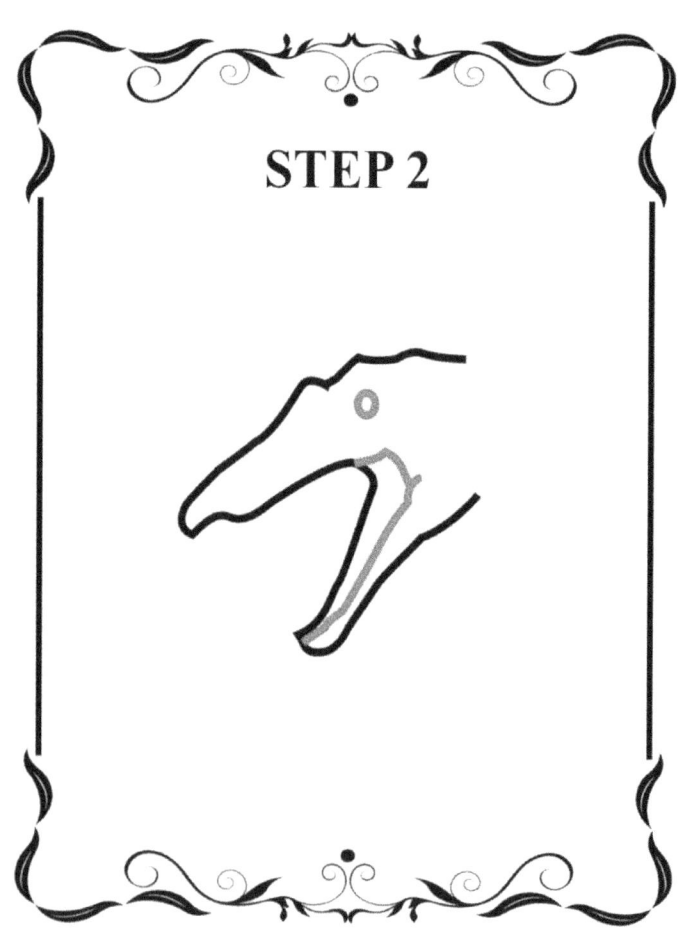

STEP 3

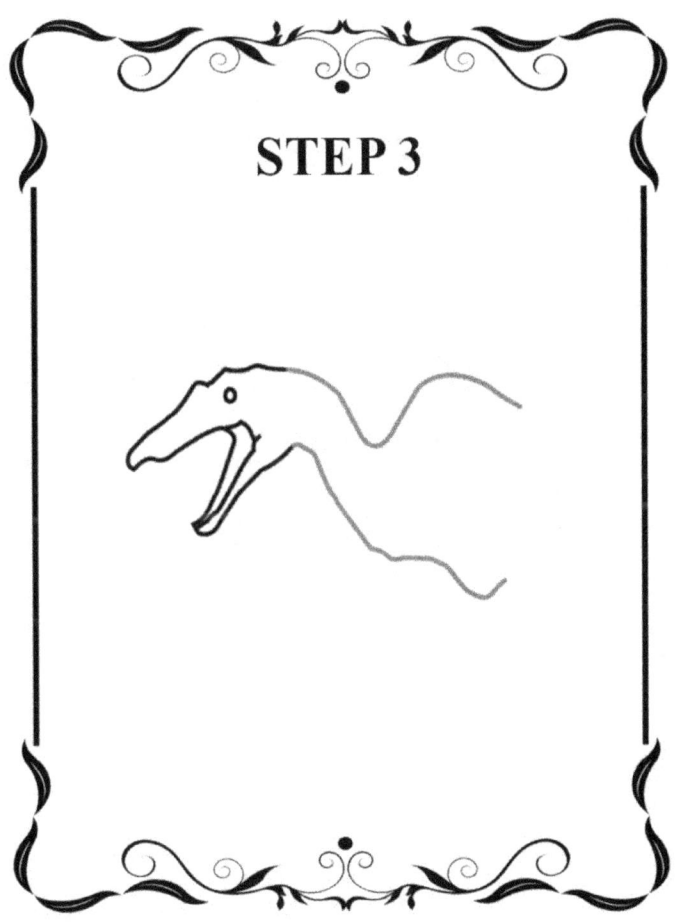

STEP 4

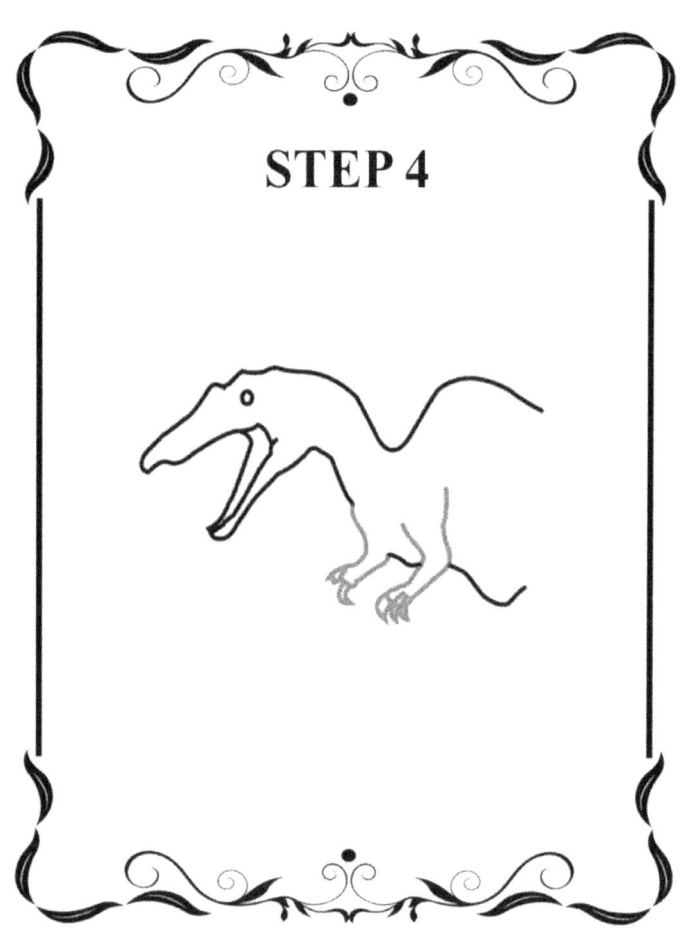

STEP 5

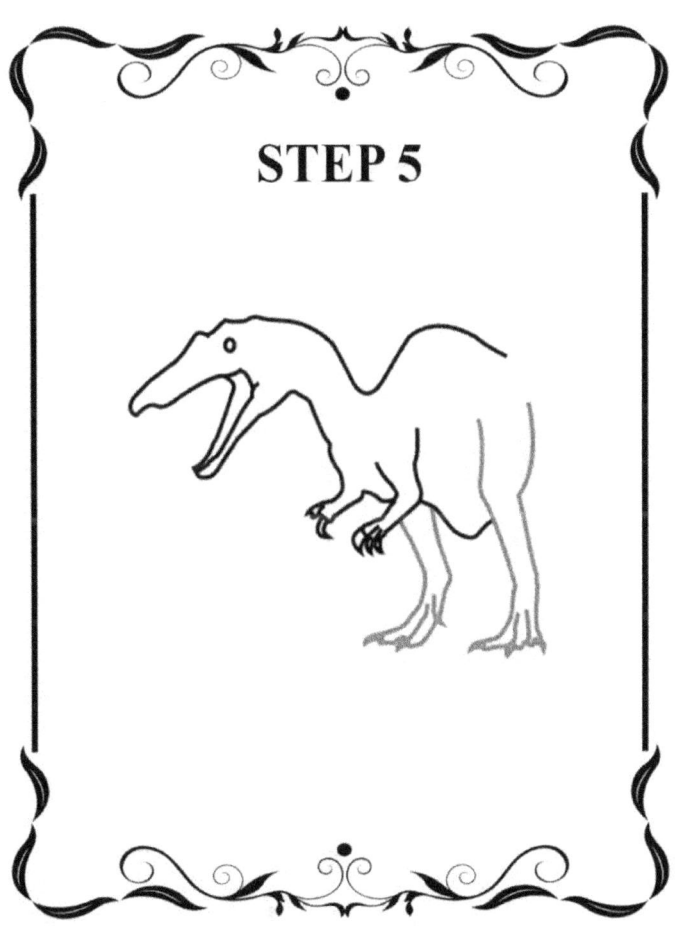

STEP 6

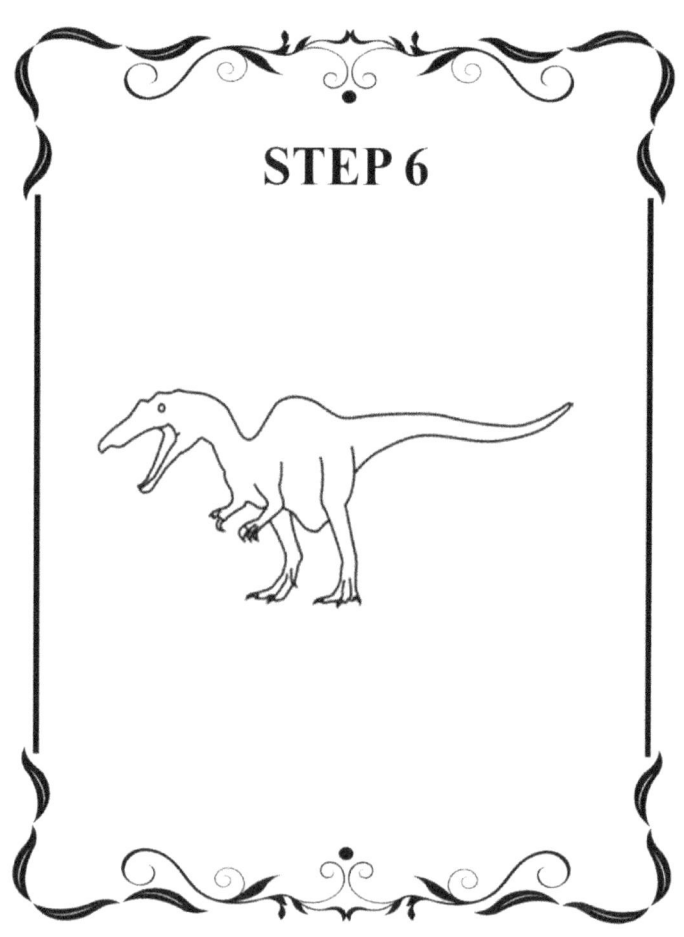

CARNOTAURUS

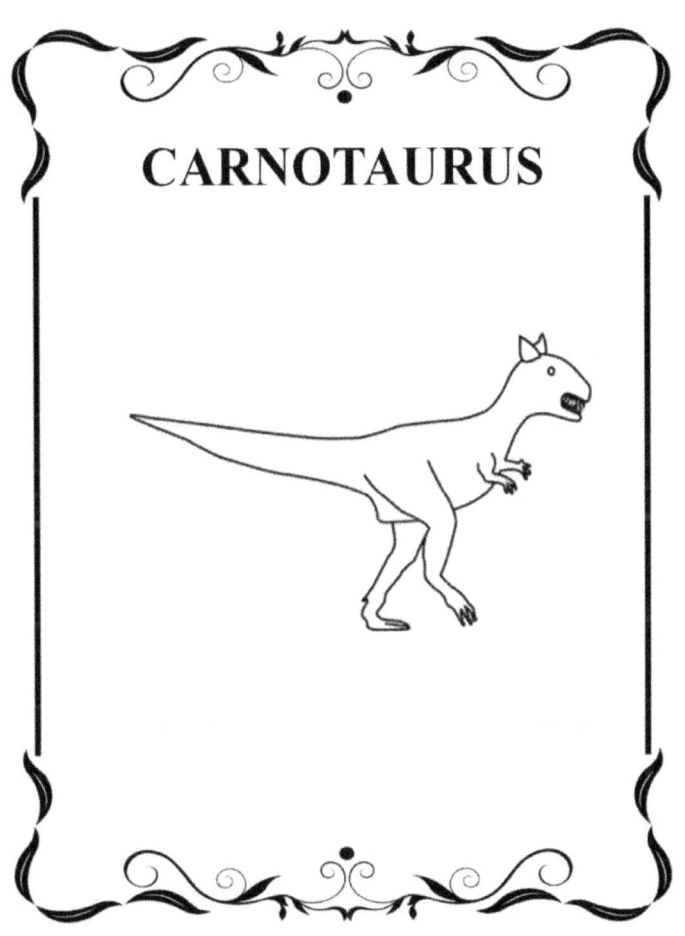

STEP 1

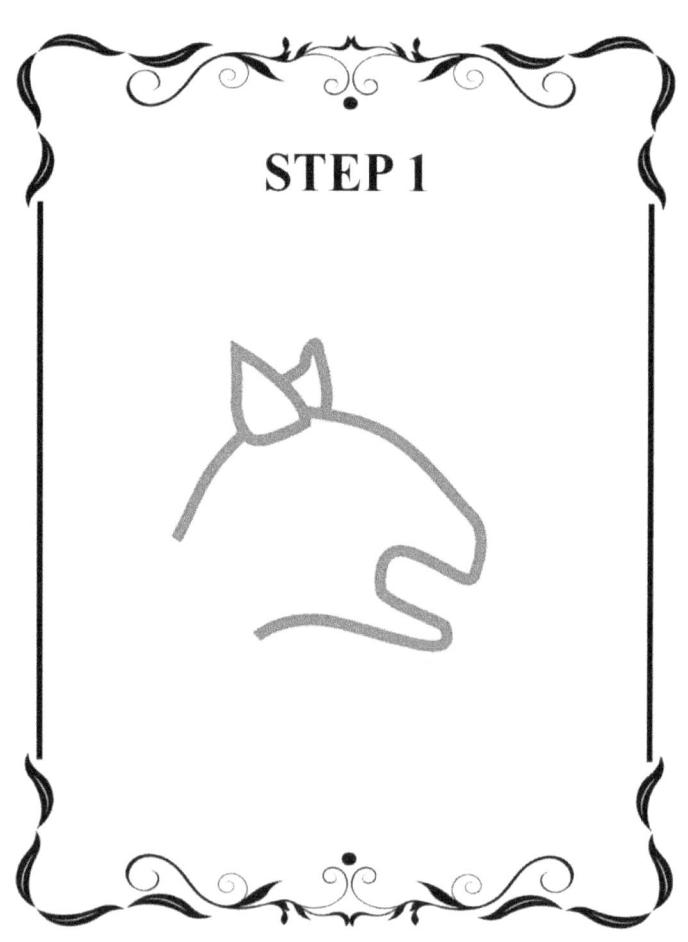

STEP 2

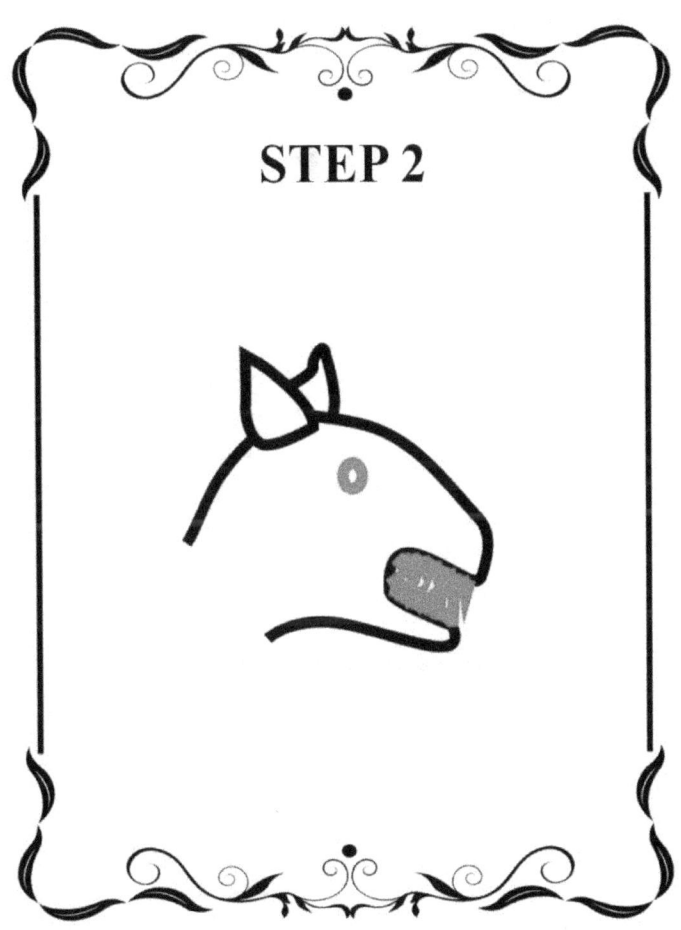

STEP 3

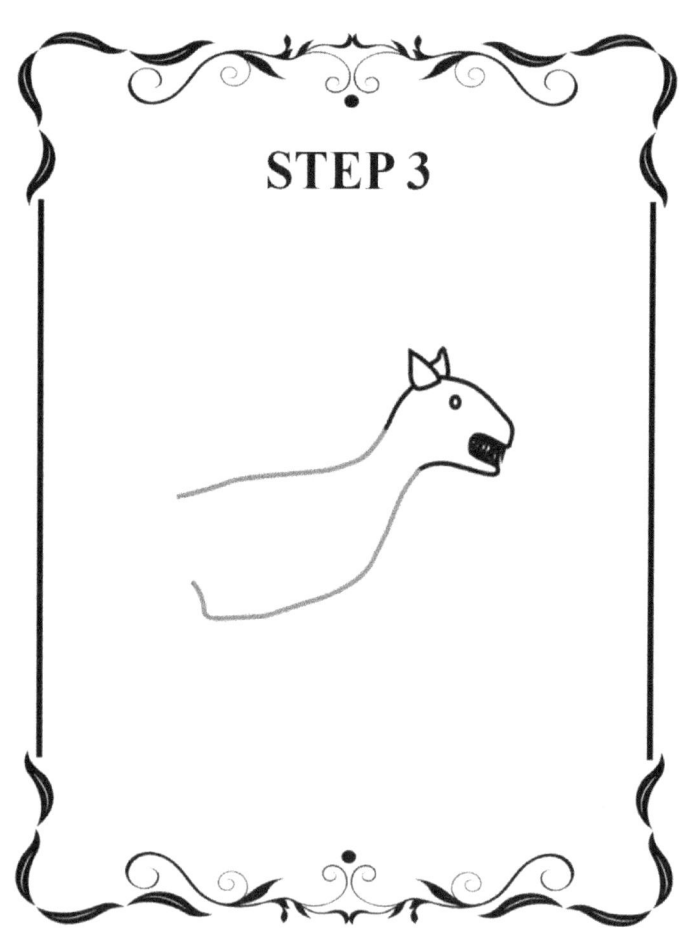

STEP 4

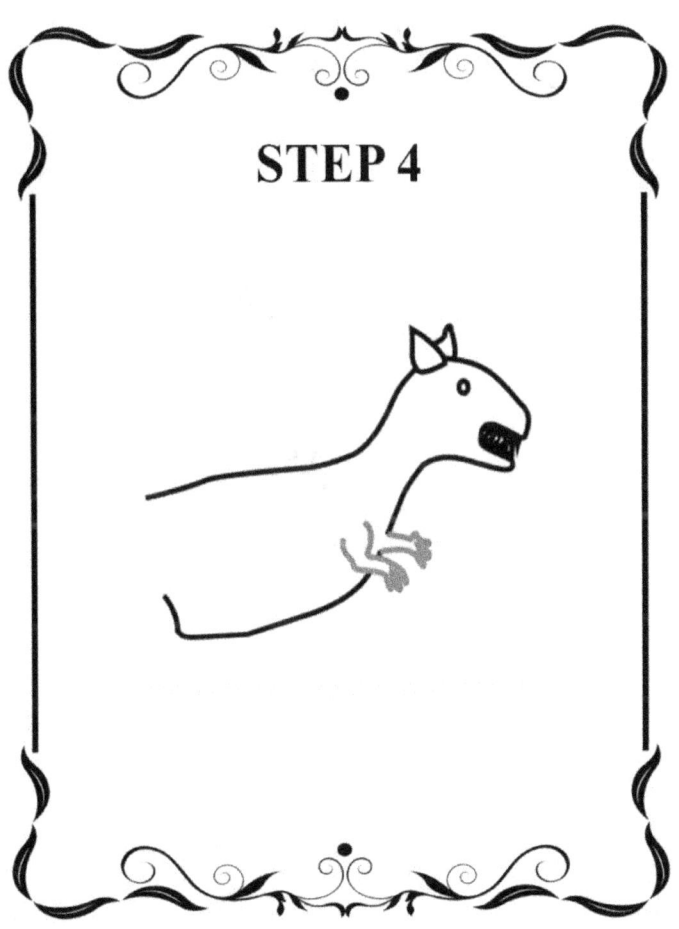

STEP 5

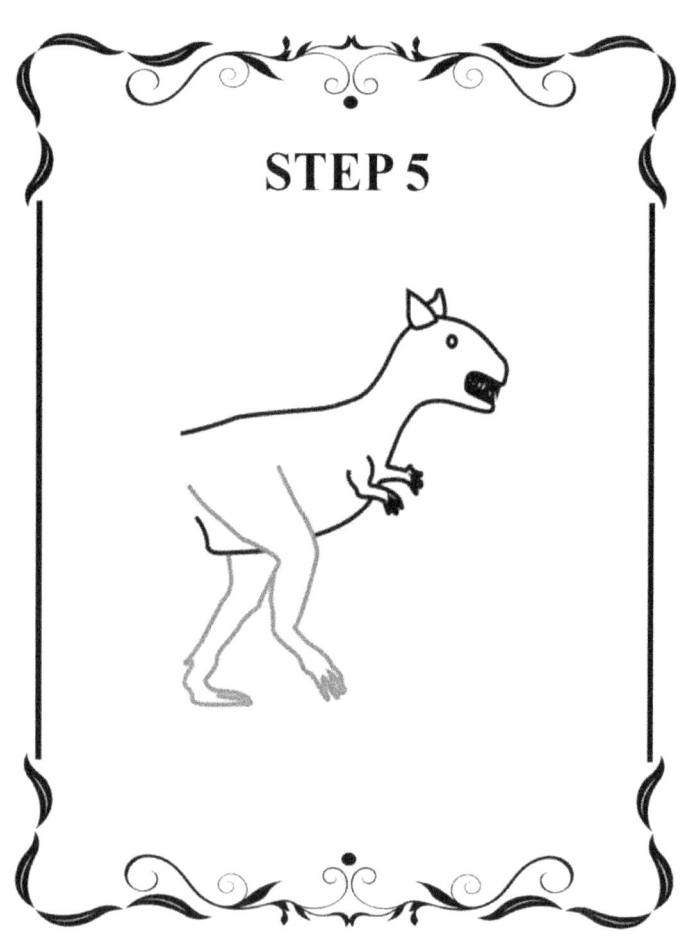

STEP 6

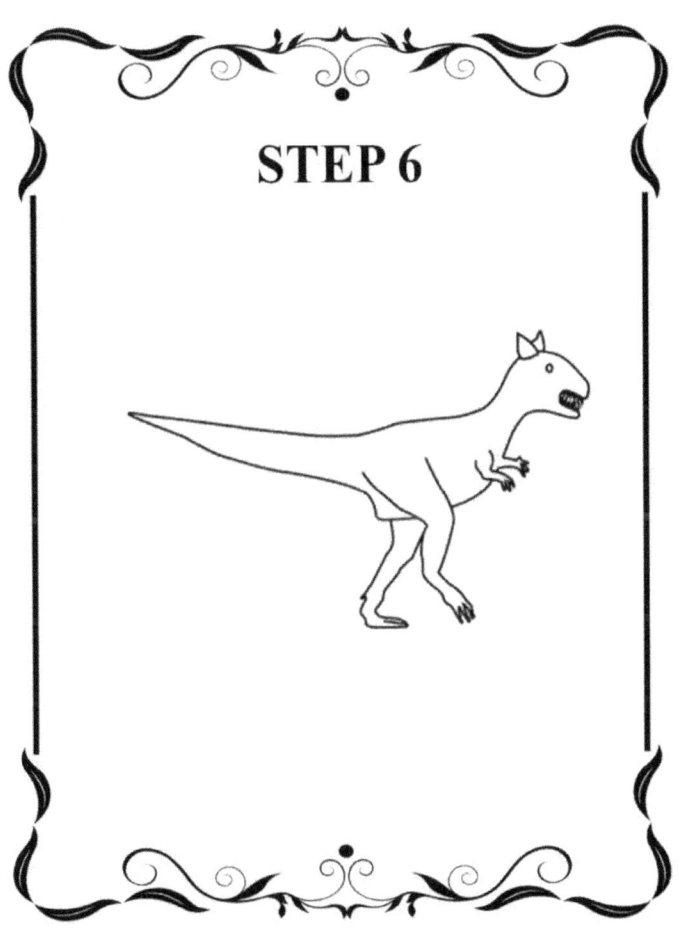

CERATOSAURUS

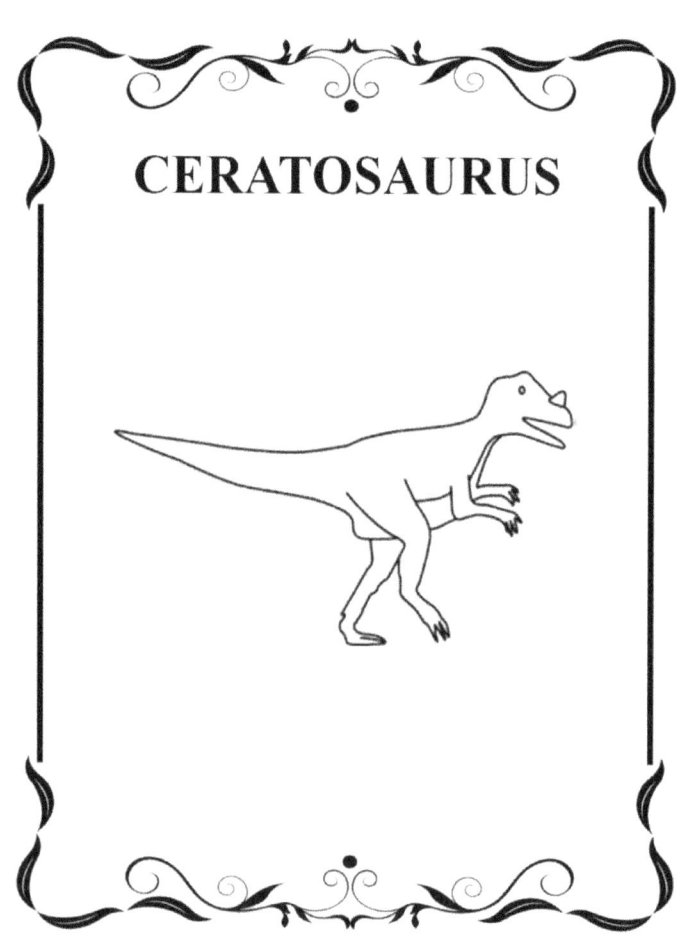

STEP 1

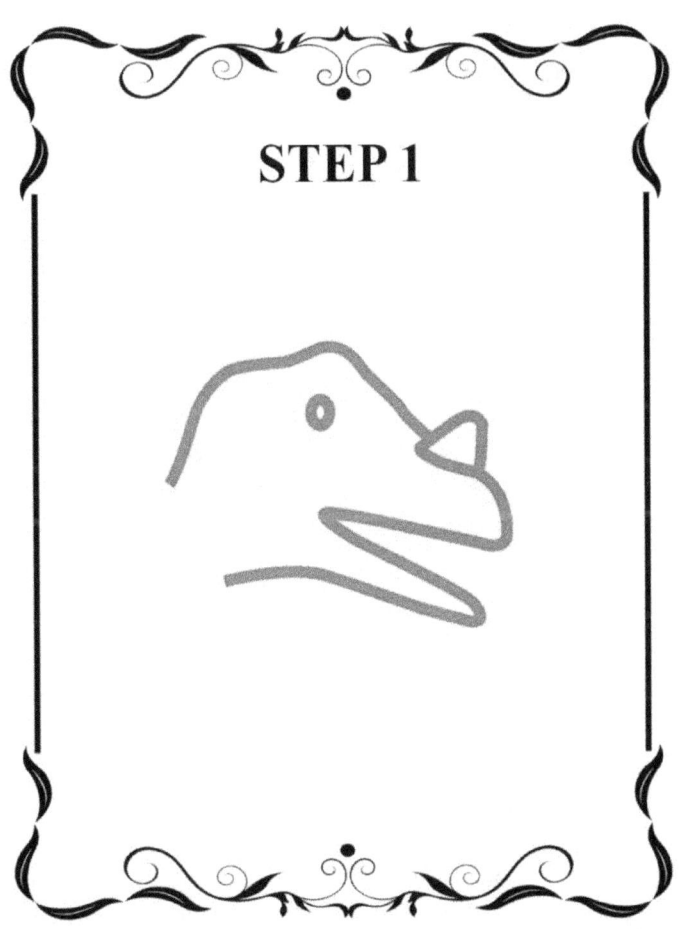

STEP 2

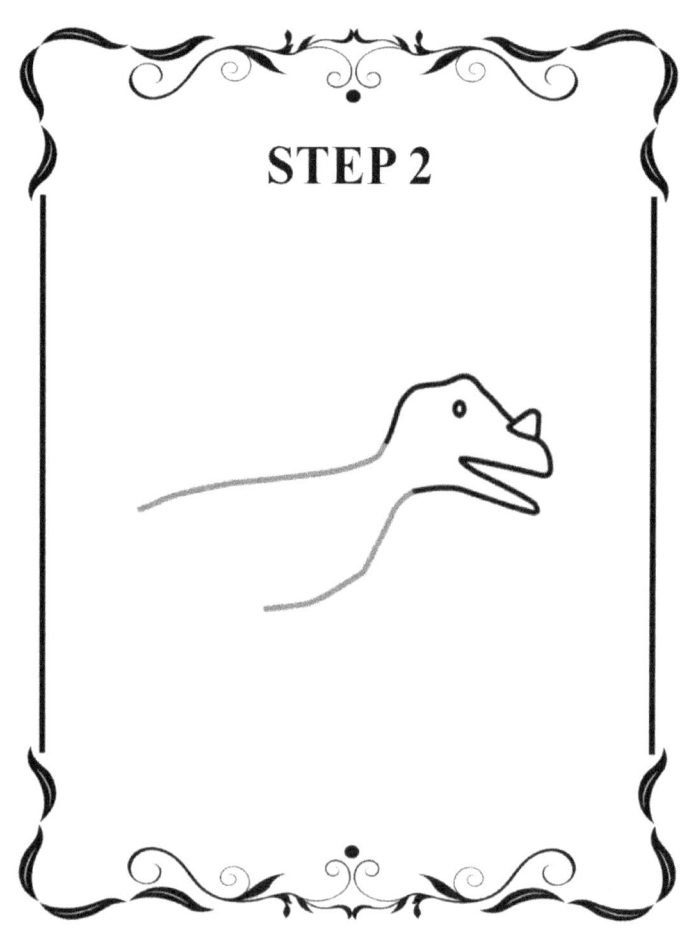

STEP 3

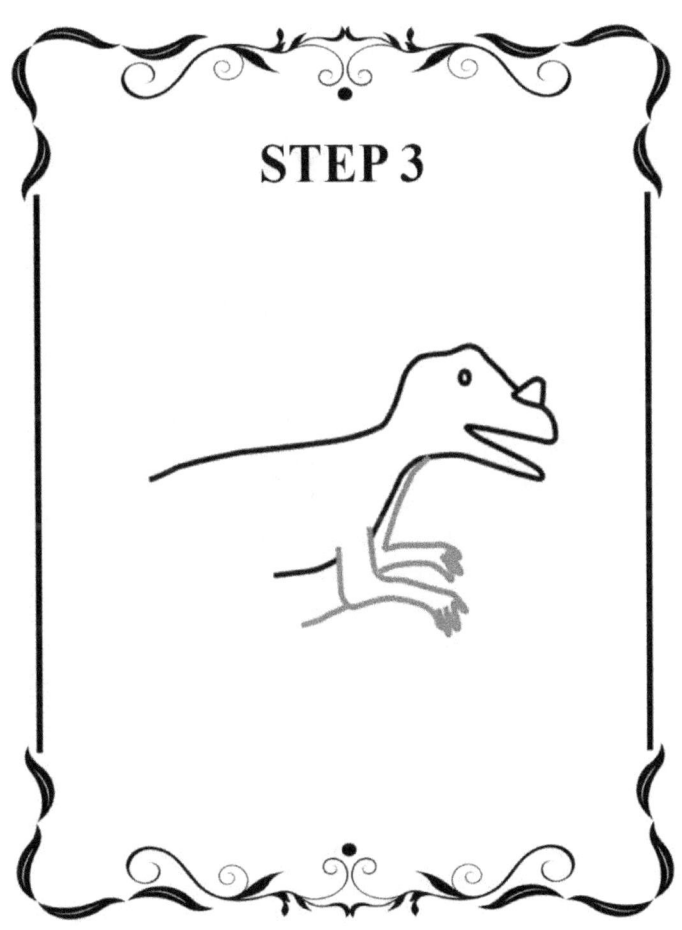

STEP 4

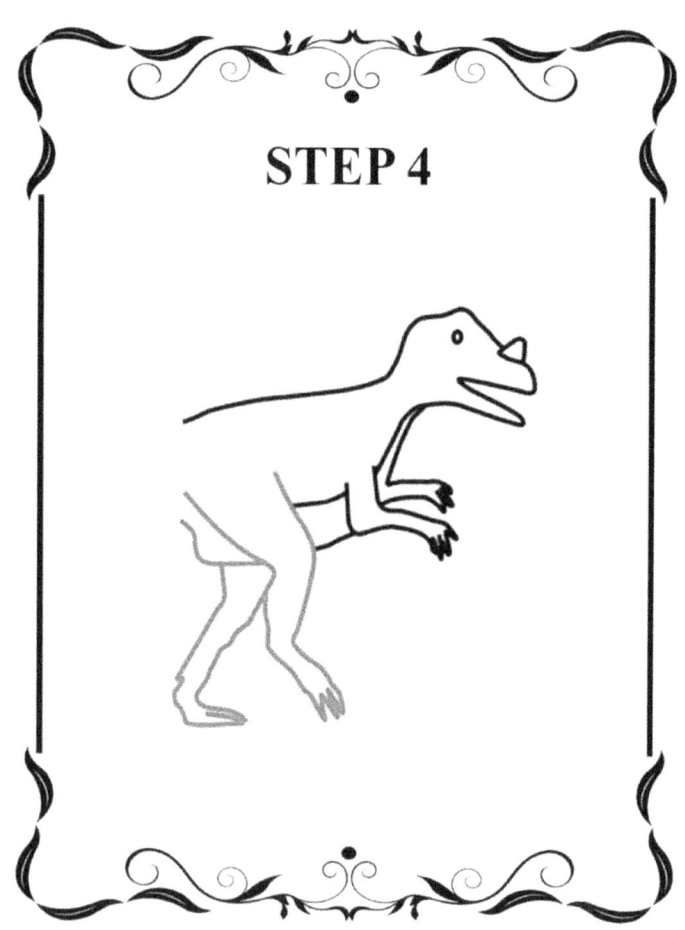

STEP 5

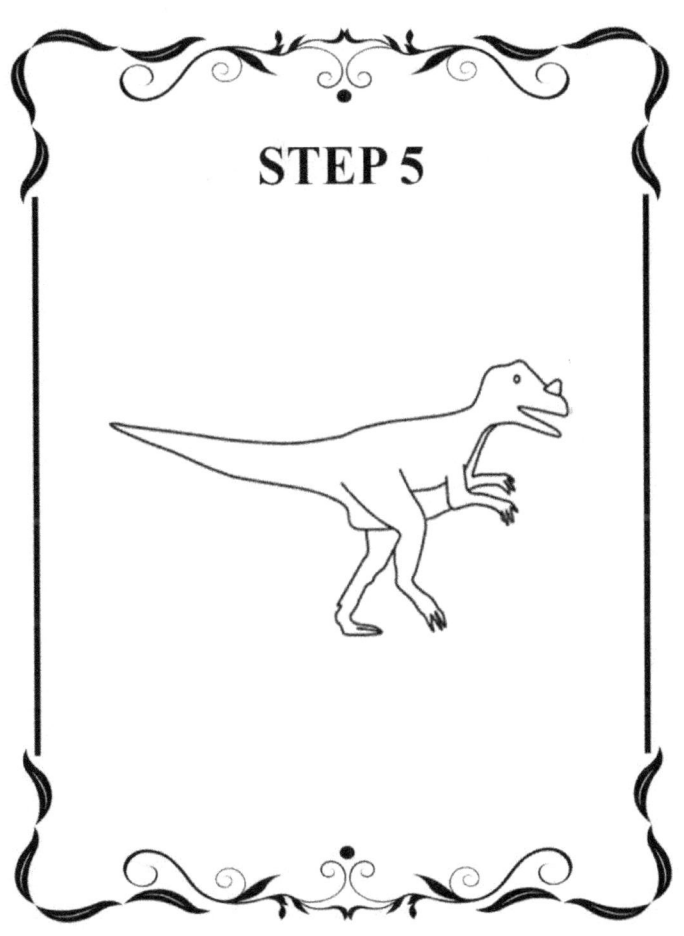

SPINOSAURUS

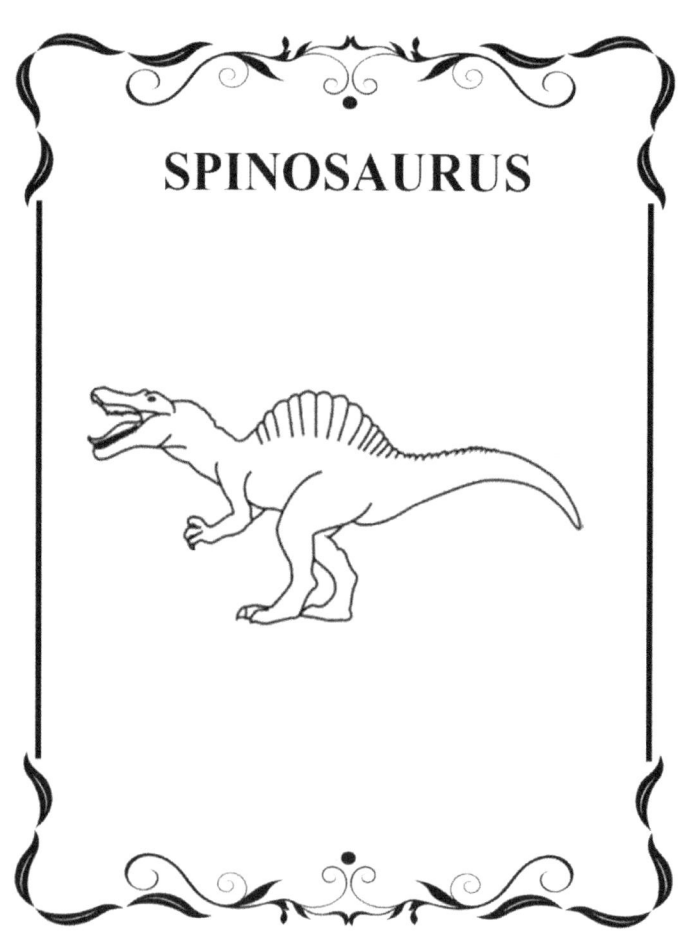

STEP 1

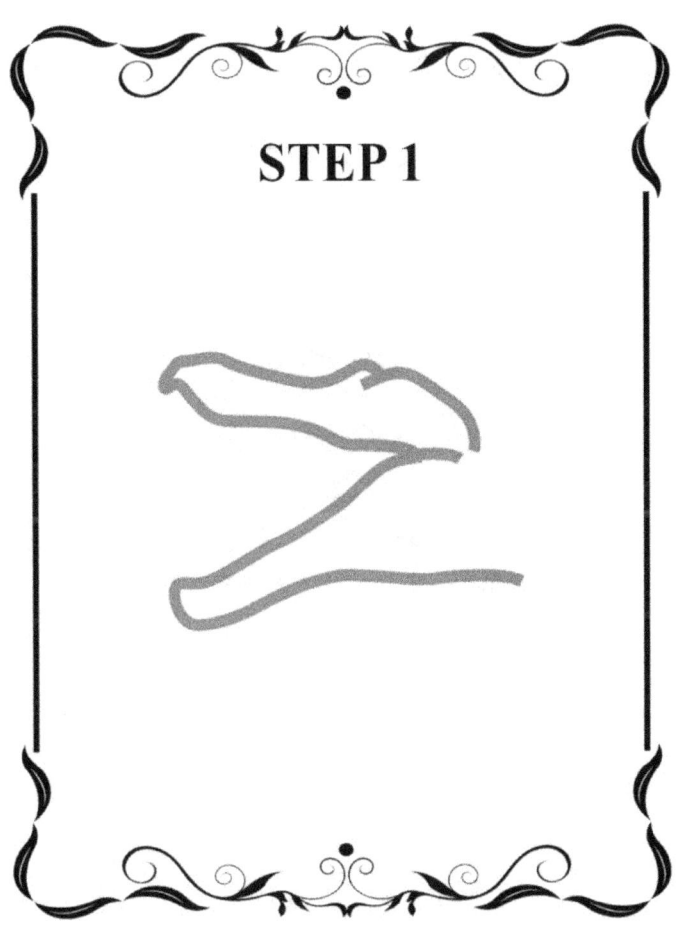

STEP 2

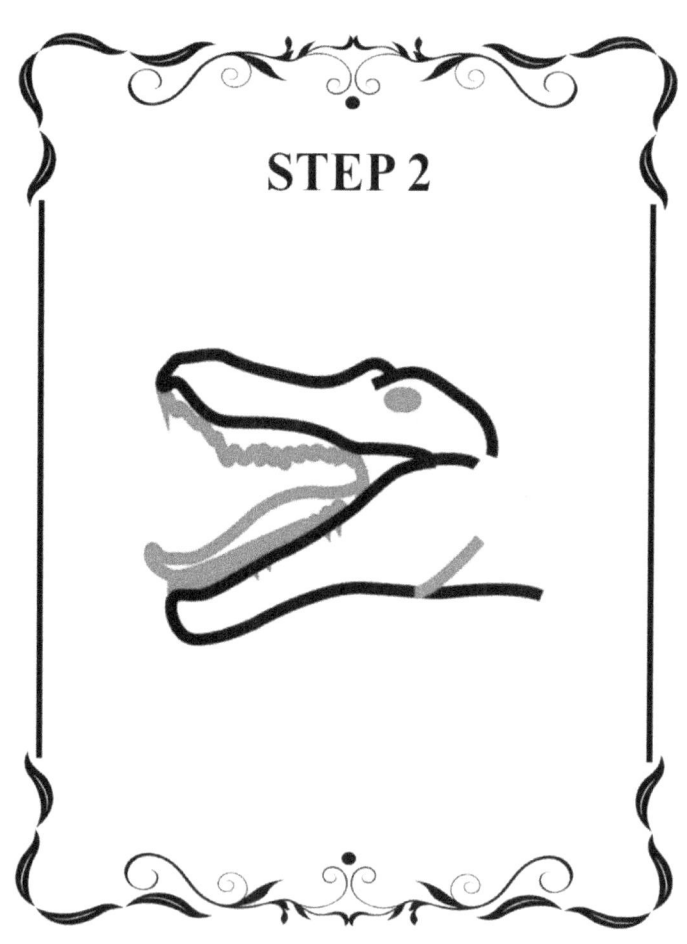

STEP 3

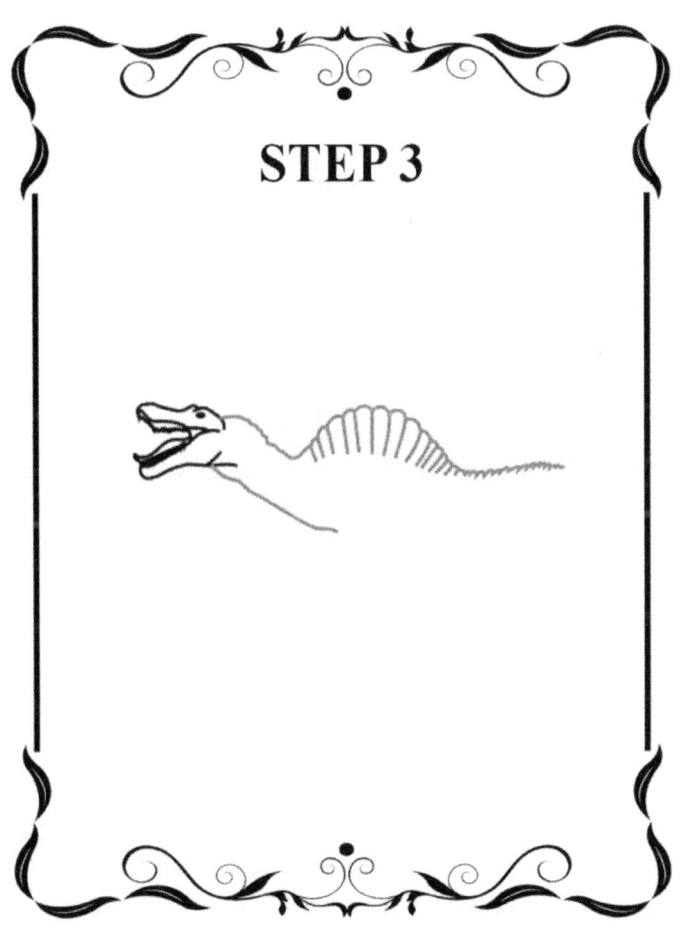

STEP 4

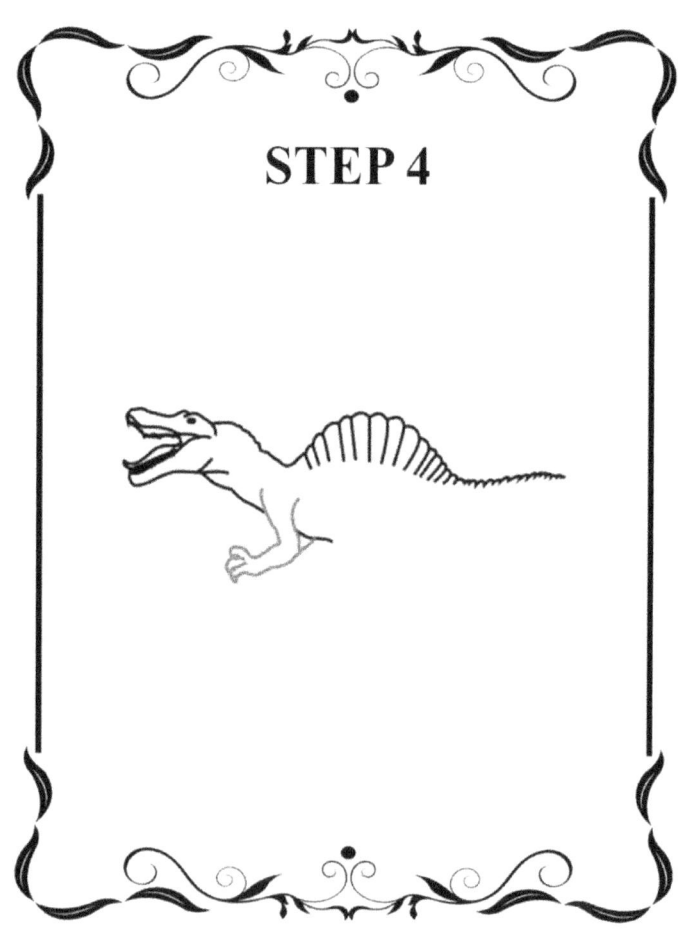

STEP 5

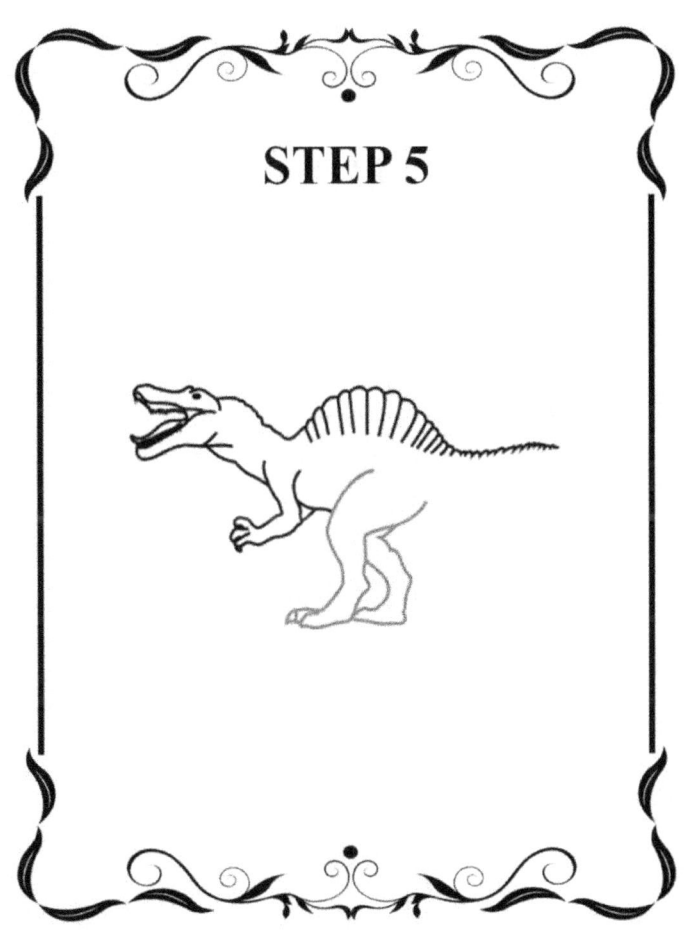

STEP 6

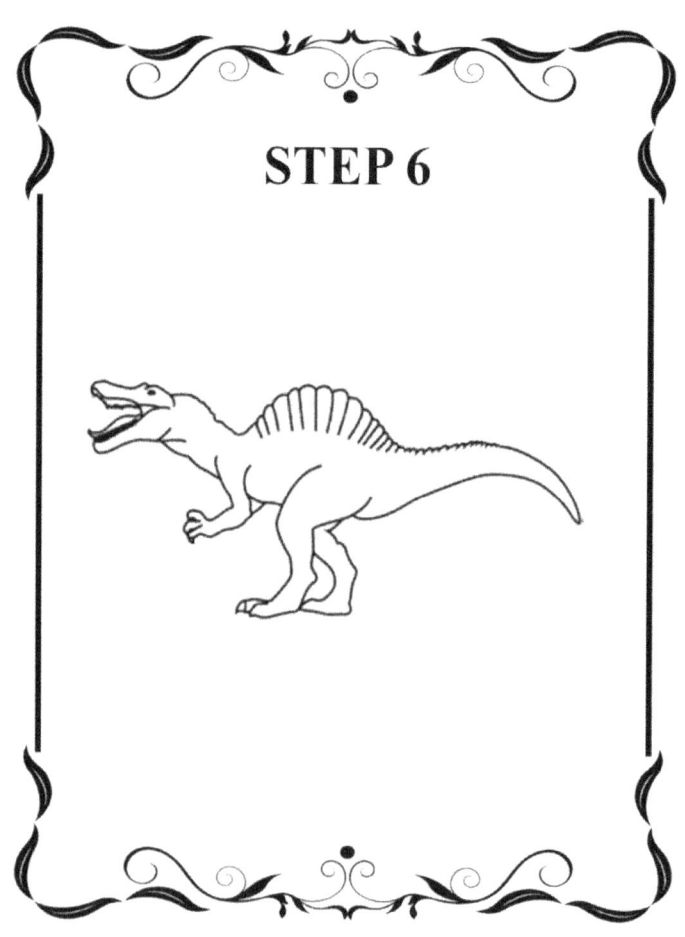

STEGOSAURUS

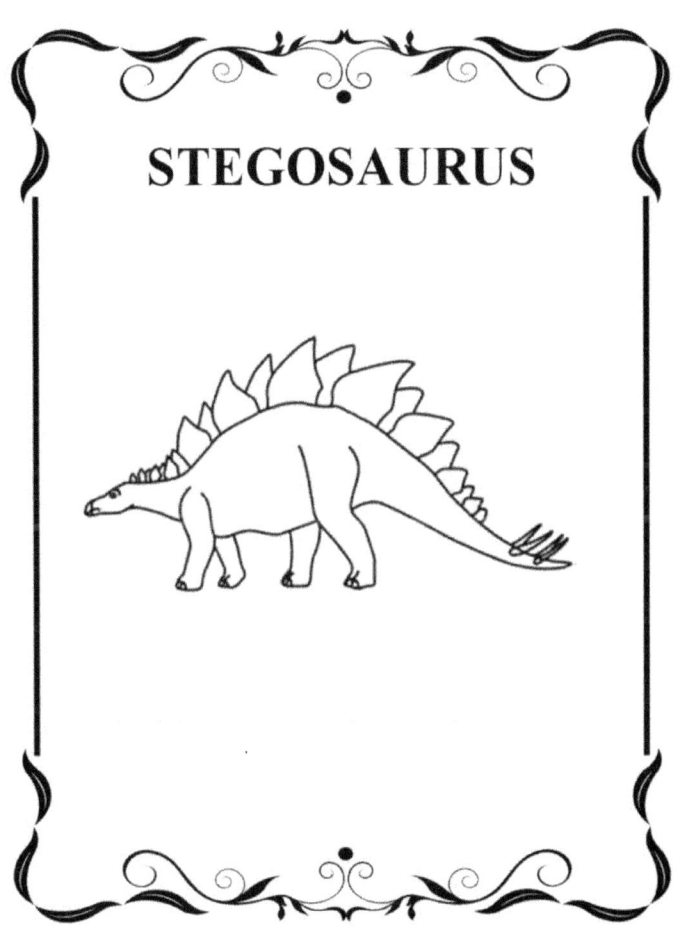

STEP 1

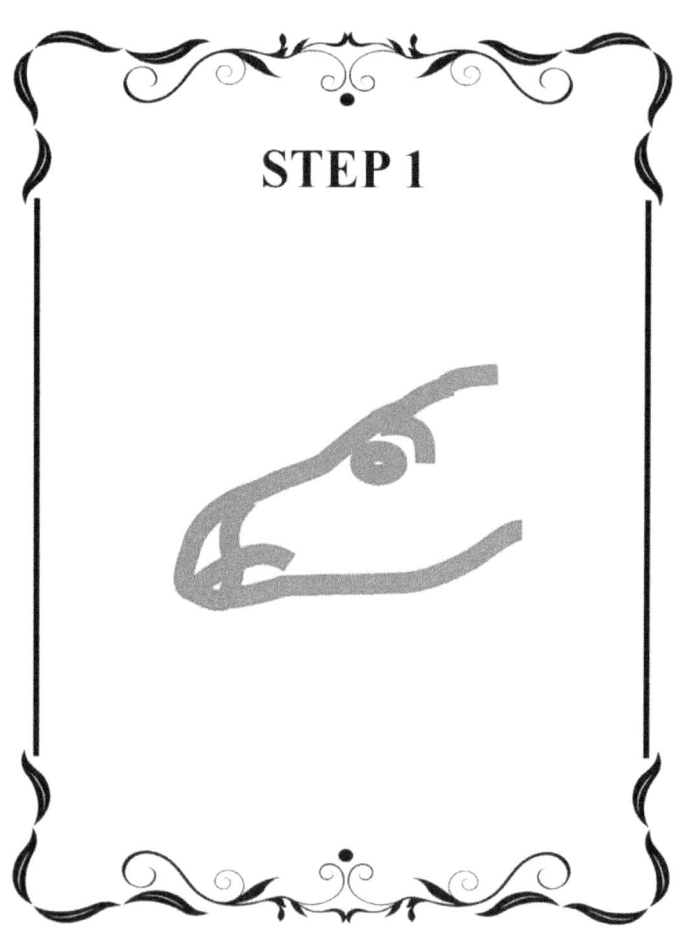

STEP 2

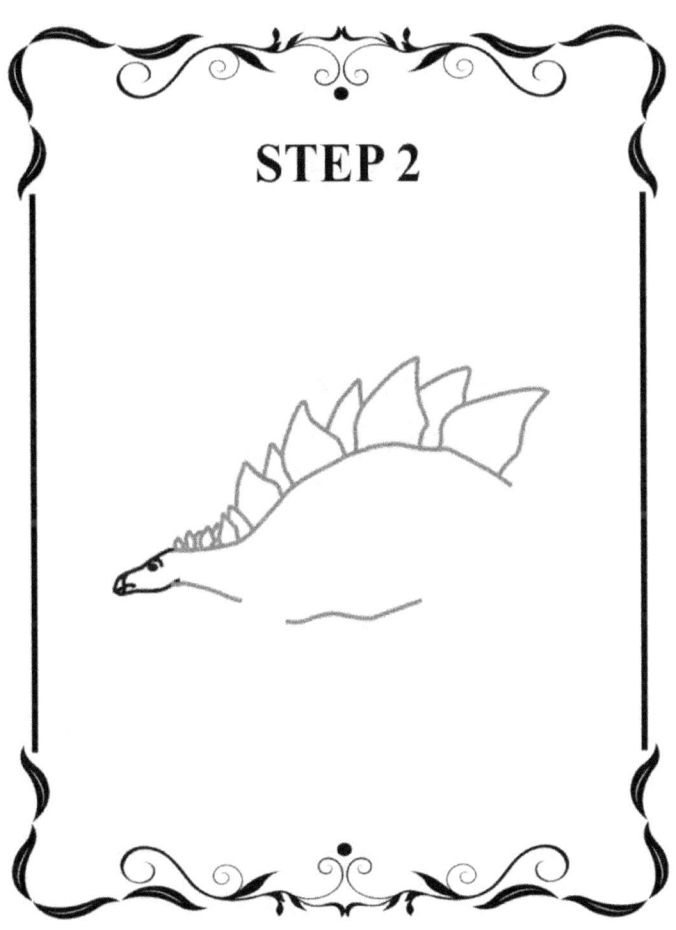

STEP 3

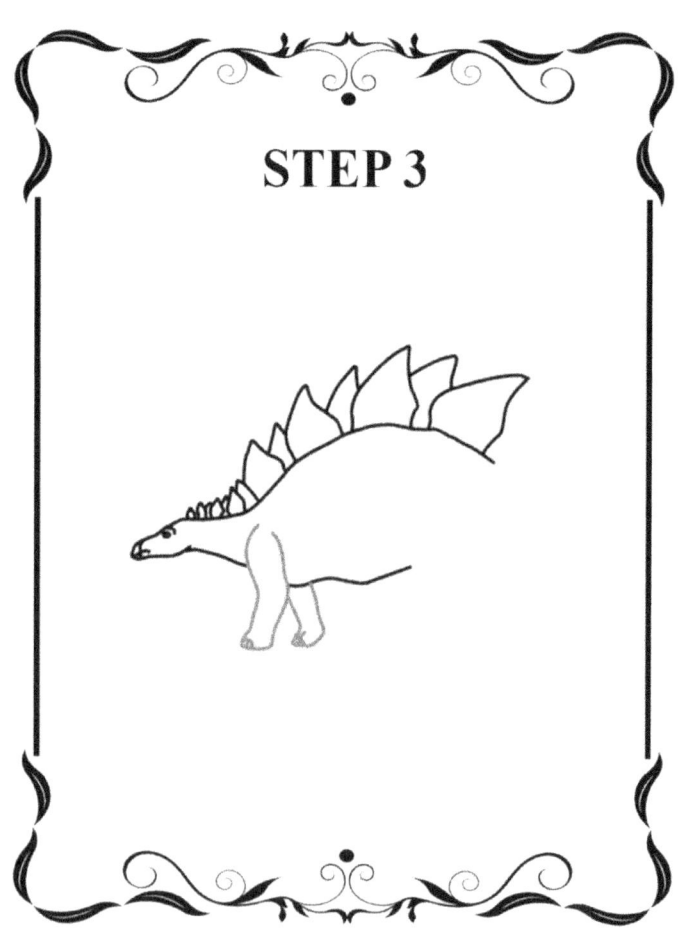

STEP 4

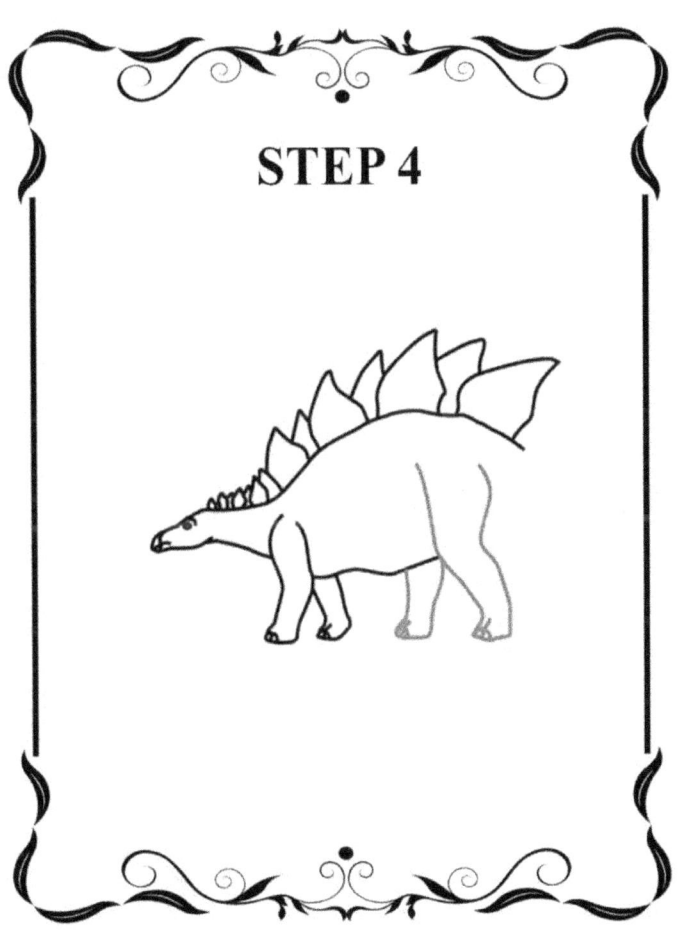

STEP 5

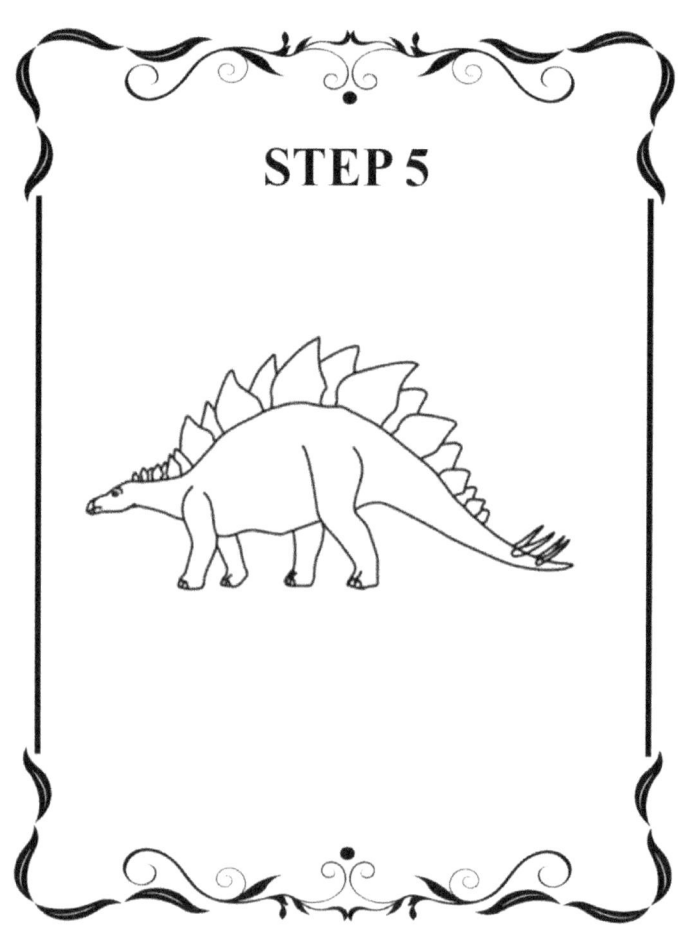

www.ingramcontent.com/pod-product-compliance
Lightning Source LLC
Chambersburg PA
CBHW071637170526
45166CB00003B/1346